The Story of Dunes

SAND ON THE MOVE

Roy A. Gallant

A FIRST BOOK

FRANKLIN WATTS
A Division of Grolier Publishing

New York ▌ London ▌ Hong Kong ▌ Sydney
Danbury, Connecticut

For Martha

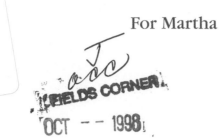

Illustrations © by Lloyd Birmingham.
Photographs ©: Photo Researchers: cover bottom left, 12 (Ray Ellis), 23 (Tom McHugh), 28, 38, 39, 42, 43 (Mark Newman), 30, 31 (George Ranalli), 51 (J.H. Robinson), cover top right (K.H. Switak); Superstock, Inc.: 9, 26; Visuals Unlimited: 7 left, 16, 17 (Jon Bertsch), 45 (Bayard Brattstrom), 1, 20, 21 (Gerald & Buff Corsi), 53 (Clint Farlinger), 14 (Ross Frid), 50 (Carlyn Galati), 46 (John Gerlach), 5 (Tim Hauf), chapter openers, cover bottom right (R. Knolan Benfield, Jr.), 33, 41 (Link), cover top left 37 (Joe McDonald), 48 (Jim Merli), 47 (Glenn Oliver), 8 (Doug Sokell), 35 (Jane Thomas).

Library of Congress Cataloging-in-Publication Data

Gallant, Roy A.
    Sand on the move: the story of dunes / Roy A. Gallant
    p.   cm. — (A First book)
    Includes bibliographical references and index.
    Summary: Discusses the different types of sand dunes, how they form and move, the destruction they can cause, and the animal and plant life they support.
        ISBN 0-531-20334-4 (lib. bdg.)   0-531-15889-6 (pbk.)
        1. Sand dunes—Juvenile literature.   [1. Sand dunes.]
    I. Title.   II. Series.
    GB632. G35   1997
    551. 3'75—dc21   96-52382
                                                                              CIP
                                                                               AC

CONTENTS

Introduction
THE WONDER OF DUNES

For centuries, a forest of oak trees lived on California's Channel Islands. Then, about 600 years ago, the area experienced a severe drought along with strong winds that lasted for many years. The winds blew millions of tons of sand off the beaches and piled it into large *sand dunes*. Over time, the winds pushed the dunes farther and farther inland.

Gradually, the mighty trees were covered by the marching sand dunes. Although the trees died, they did not fall over. They were held upright by the sand packed tightly around them.

Eventually, the drought ended and torrential rains began to fall. Water drained down through the sand until it reached the solid ground below the dunes. A variety of plant seeds carried by the wind took root in the wet dunes. Soon, the area looked like rolling hills covered with grasses and other plants, but the buried forest lay below it all.

Where a forest of oak trees once stood are only "stumps" of calcite, the work of time and sand. These forest remains are on California's San Miguel Island, Channel Islands National Park.

The new, lush vegetation made a perfect feast for invading land snails. With no natural enemies on the islands, and with plenty of food, the snails reproduced very rapidly. Soon, there were so many snails that they ate all of the plant cover. Then, since there was nothing left to eat, the snails died. All that was left behind were their shells.

As the area was exposed to the bright sun and the rain, the snails' limestone shells began to break down. Some of the dissolved limestone seeped into the ground and mixed with the sand grains. Layer after layer of this cement-like material coated the trunks and branches of the buried trees. Eventually, each tree wore a tough limestone jacket.

Because there was no vegetation to hold the sand dunes in place, the strong winds that had originally buried the oak forest now began to uncover it. In time, the entire ancient forest was exposed. But, now instead of trees, the forest consisted of cement-like forms wherever a tree had been. All the structures were hollow because their wood had long ago rotted away.

This is just one of the amazing stories of how sand dunes change the land. Read on to learn how the wind creates sand dunes and then pushes them across the landscape. Along the way you will discover where the sand comes from and why dunes come in many different shapes and sizes. You will also find out that sand dunes are not just heaps of sand. Dunes, especially those found in deserts, are home to many unusual animals and plants. To survive in such a hot, dry, harsh environment, these *organisms* have developed all sorts of special traits.

Right: Death Valley National Monument in California has some of the nation's most spectacular sand dunes.

FROM ROCK TO DUNE

Sand dunes are found in deserts and along the coasts of oceans, lakes, and rivers. A sand dune may be as small as an anthill or as tall as a 15-story building. Although sand dunes come in a variety of sizes and shapes, all are formed the same way. Every dune is a pile of sand built up by the wind.

FROM ROCK TO SAND

Most of the sand you see today was once part of a rock. Rocks may seem indestructible, but they aren't. You can hammer a rock into fine sandlike particles. Nature has several ways of changing rock into sand.

When rocks are exposed to heat, cold, water, and wind, they are often broken into pieces. The most coarse pieces become gravel, smaller pieces become sand, and the finest pieces become silt.

When rocks are exposed to crashing waves or whipping winds, they begin to erode and crumble. And when water flows into a rock's nooks and crannies, and then freezes, the rock may split into many pieces. Rocks may also break up when they bump into one another.

The scorching heat of the day and freezing cold of the night cause rocks to expand and shrink. As they do, they are broken apart and become sand.

When rocks break down, they form gravel, sand, or silt. Most sand grains are tiny pieces of a mineral called *quartz*, or *silicon dioxide*, that are loosened when granite breaks apart.

The sand on some beaches and deserts consists of other materials. In certain areas of the New Mexican

8

The gleaming whiteness of the dunes of White Sands, New Mexico comes from sand grains of nearly pure gypsum. Farther north, this desert is dominated by less dazzling quartz sand grains.

desert, most of the sand is made of the mineral *gypsum*. The black sand that forms the beaches of Hawaii is made of tiny grains of *basalt*, or hardened volcanic lava.

The dazzling white beaches of many Caribbean Islands are made of *calcite*. This white sand consists of crushed seashells and coral. Seven Mile Beach in Dongara, Australia, and the beaches of Japan's Ryukyu Islands are also made of calcite sand.

9

Sometimes, the plants that grow on calcite dunes have limestone casings around their stems. These *lime tubes* are made of calcite that dissolves when it rains. When the raindrops on the plants evaporate, the calcite is left behind and forms a jacket around the stems.

Sometimes, a sand dune contains pieces of a material that forms when lightning strikes the sand. The lightning's heat melts the quartz grains. When they solidify, they form small tubelike pieces of glass called *fulgurite*.

FROM THE MOUNTAINS TO THE SEA

Most of the sand that ends up in dunes begins as part of a mountain. As the edges of the parent rock crumble, the pieces are washed downhill into a river or stream. These pieces are broken into smaller and smaller bits as they bounce and roll over the stream bottom. Although the sand grains may be briefly trapped in a small quiet pool, or in a hollow at the base of a boulder, most end up in the ocean. Along the way, the grains may be polished by chemicals in the flowing water. It takes about 1 million years for a medium-sized river to wash a grain of sand 100 miles (160 km) downstream.

Sometimes, the wind picks up the grains before they wash into a stream and carries them to the ocean. When this happens, the grains are not polished and usually have a frosted look. Sand carried by the wind may complete its journey to the ocean in just a few hours or a few days. It depends on how strong the wind is and how far the sand grains are from the ocean.

As sand is carried down a river, waves wash some of it up onto the riverbank. When the grains dry out, they too may be picked up by the wind and blown away. This sand may take much longer to reach the ocean—or it may never get there.

For the most part, however, the sand that starts out as mountain rock does eventually makes it to one of the world's oceans. This process has been happening for millions of years—ever since Earth's surface formed.

Over the centuries, conditions on Earth have changed a great deal. There have been periods when the planet was hotter than it is today and eras when it was colder. During the hotter periods, some of Earth's oceans and shallow inland seas dried up. Only their sandy floors were left behind. Today these huge areas of ancient ocean floor are called deserts.

Most of the world's sandy deserts—such as those in Mexico, the Middle East, northern Africa, and central Australia—lie close to the equator. These areas receive less than 10 inches (25 cm) of rainfall a year.

Desert sands come in many colors. This red sand desert is in Saudi Arabia.

In general, a desert is any area that receives only a small amount of moisture. The desert regions of Utah, Colorado, and Arizona get little rain because the Sierra Nevada mountains of California cut off the rain-rich winds that blow off the Pacific Ocean. Because the Andes mountain range in South America also blocks moist ocean winds, there is a large desert area in western Argentina.

HOW A DUNE FORMS

Sand along an ocean beach, or part of a desert, is always at the mercy of the wind. Once sand has been picked up by the wind, it will go wherever the wind carries it. At some point, something will happen to make the wind drop its load of sand. However, scientists studying a particular sand dune cannot always figure out what that *something* was.

Sometimes a dune begins to form when the wind encounters an object. For example, when wind blows

When wind encounters an object, such as a rock, it drops its load of sand. As time passes, the sand piles up and a dune begins to form.

Glacial ice left this mountain of dune sand along the shore of Lake Michigan.

against a small bush or a rock about the size of a basketball, it is forced to change direction and move around the object. As it hits the object, the wind then drops many of its sand particles in one spot. Before long, a small mound of wind-blown sand piles up in front of the bush or rock.

As the sand keeps piling up, it blocks more and more wind. Before long, the bush or rock is completely buried in sand. At this point, the wind may begin to change the dune's shape. It may make the dune larger by adding more sand to it, or it may push the dune along the ground. The location of the dune can affect how the wind shapes it.

Many of the dunes we see today were formed by ice. Most of the sand that makes up the dunes along the southern shore of Lake Michigan and the northeastern coast of the United States was dumped by glaciers at the end of the last ice age. As the glaciers extended farther and farther toward the equator, they scraped Earth's surface, picking up boulders, gravel, and sand. When the glacier melted, the rock and sand was left behind.

In the case of Michigan's dunes, the invading glacier was 1 mile (1. 6 km) or more thick and contained untold tons of rubble. When the glacier melted, it left piles of sand and gravel 300 feet (90 m) tall.

The wind patterns in California's Death Valley create a chaos of sand dunes. But notice that the small wavy pattern from one dune formation to the next is the same. This indicates a single prevailing wind direction.

2

Even though most sand dunes are made of the same material and form in the same way, they vary widely in appearance. They may be long and straight or look like a crescent moon. They may look like ocean waves or a star. What a sand dune looks like depends on the direction and strength of the wind that created it.

Sometimes dunes form in areas where the wind almost always blows in the same direction. When this happens in a desert, the sand may look like the ocean's wavy surface—but with all the waves frozen in place. These wavy sand dunes are

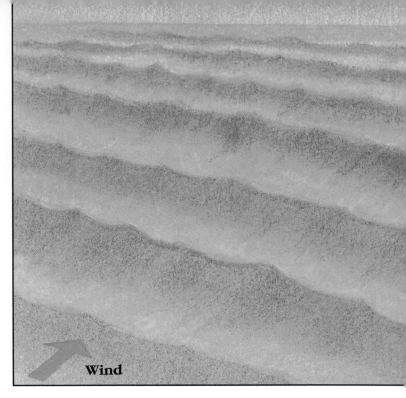

Transverse dunes are created by light winds that blow in just one direction.

Wind

called *transverse dunes*. Transverse dunes are actually more common inland from beaches than they are in desert regions.

Because the winds that form these dunes are not very strong, transverse dunes are usually made up of very fine sand. The sand is blown up one side, or *face*, of the dune and then tumbles down over the other side. In some cases, a series of transverse dunes may form one after another. This group of dunes may creep along like ocean waves in slow motion.

A *barchan dune* is shaped like a crescent. The two tips of the dune point in the direction in which the wind is blowing, and the dune moves along slowly in the same direction as the wind.

The sand of a barchan dune is blown up the side facing the wind and swept over the curved top. Then it slides down the steep opposite side, which is called the *slipface*. This wind action causes the dune to creep along a few inches a day with its crescent "horns" pointed forward. Small barchan dunes travel about twice as fast as larger ones.

Barchan dunes are shaped like a crescent with tips that point in the direction the wind is blowing.

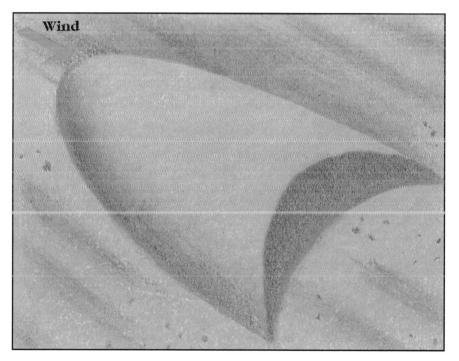

Wind

Wind-blown sand is pushed along the gently sloping face of this dune and then tumbles over the crest and down the steep slipface. This barchan dune is in the Mesquite Flat Dunes area of Death Valley National Monument in California.

Barchan dunes are generally 30 to 100 feet (9 to 30 m) high. The distance from one crescent tip to the other may be as much as 1,200 feet (365 m). These dunes are usually found in places where the ground is hard and flat, and not much sand is present. Like transverse dunes, they often form in groups.

Scientists do not fully understand the earliest stages of barchan dune formation. Some believe that both sides, or *slopes*, of the dune may initially be rounded, so that the dune looks like a large mound. This type of large sand mound is common in Canada.

Like a barchan dune, a parabolic dune is shaped like the letter "U." Unlike a barchan dune, the tips point into the wind.

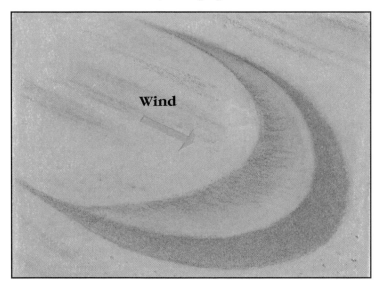

This area in Baja California features several parabolic dunes. Some, like the one in the foreground, have plants growing on them. The vegetation affects the shape the dune will have.

If these mounds continue to grow, they may eventually develop a slipface on the side that is not facing into the wind. What happens to the dunes next depends on whether they remain dry or become moist. If they remain dry, they develop into barchan dunes. But if they become moist, they form *parabolic dunes*.

Parabolic dunes, which are common along coastal areas and in the southwestern United States and throughout Canada, can be thought of as backward barchan dunes. Like barchan dunes, they are shaped like the let-

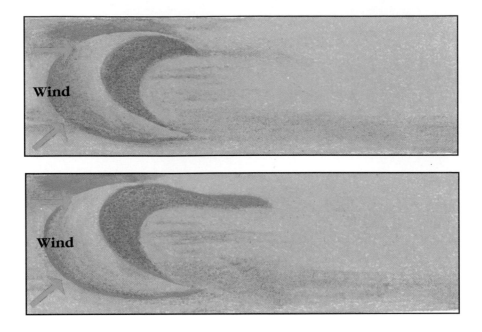

ter "U." The difference is that the tips of a parabolic dune point into the wind, rather than away from it.

The shape of some parabolic dunes seems to be influenced by patches of grasses and other plants growing on them. Any dune covered with vegetation is called a *phytogenic dune*. The roots of the dune plants hold the sand particles together, making the dunes stronger. The portion of a parabolic dune that is not covered by plants is directly exposed to the wind and can be more easily pushed along. As a result, the dune is shaped like a "U."

Longitudinal dunes are formed in locations where the wind blows mainly in one direction. But, at times, this

24

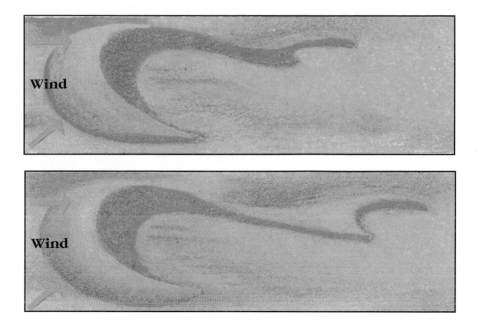

Barchan dunes may develop into longitudinal dunes if cross winds cause one tip to grow more quickly than the other. Longitudinal dunes often form in rows.

direction may change. These dunes may stretch out for miles in the direction the wind is blowing. They are the largest of all dunes. Some longitudinal dunes in the Middle East are 700 feet (213 m) high and almost 1 mile (1. 6 km) wide at the base. Like parabolic dunes, longitudinal dunes may grow out of barchan dunes when one tip grows faster than the other. Eventually, the rapidly growing tip begins to collect sand that moves around the shorter tip.

The sharply defined crest of this dune in Death Valley, California clearly separates the steep and highlighted slipface from the gently sloping face, which is marked by deep ridges formed by the wind.

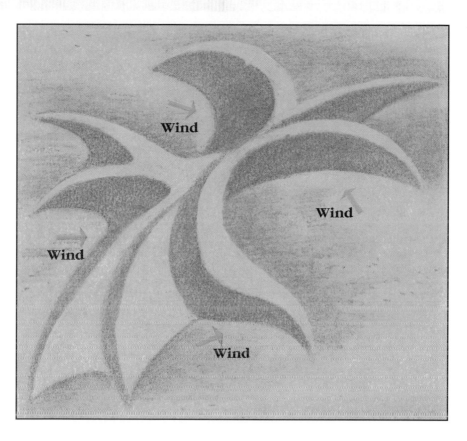

Star-shaped dunes form in areas with winds from many different directions.

Other types of dunes are formed by opposing winds. *Star-shaped dunes* can be found in deserts where winds come first from one direction then from another. In the Arabian Desert and the Sahara dunes, that look like many-pointed stars are often 300 feet (90 m) high. Star

dunes may keep their shape for hundreds of years, so they can serve as reliable desert landmarks for travelers. *S-shaped dunes* form when winds of equal intensity blow first from one direction, and then from the opposite direction.

A *barrier dune* is any type of dune that forms along an ocean beach. These dunes grow so large that they protect trees and houses along the shore against strong winds, storm waves, and flood tides. Sometimes grasses and other plants grow on these dunes.

In some cases, land developers have bulldozed barrier dunes to make room for more houses. More than once, this unwise action has exposed buildings to the destructive action of storm winds.

This beautifully-formed S-shaped dune has been built by wind blowing first from one direction then later from the opposite direction.

The shape and location of mountainous dunes, as well as small ones, are continually changed by the wind.

DUNES ON THE MOVE

3

Once a dune gains a foothold, it usually grows and, eventually, begins to creep in the same direction as the dominant wind. As sand blows up the side of the dune that is exposed to the wind, a gentle slope forms. When the sand reaches the crest of the dune, it tumbles over the top and down the other side, forming a steep slope. As you learned in Chapter 2, this steep slope is called the slipface. When the slope of the slipface becomes too steep, a layer of sand breaks free and slides down the face. In this way, the growing dune creeps forward.

31

The steepness of a dune's slipface depends on the amount of sand, the size of the grains, and the sand's moisture. A dune's moisture comes from groundwater, and the amount of groundwater depends on the climate of that area.

In deserts there is usually little groundwater available, so dunes are dry and easily blown by the wind. In other areas, the surface sand of dunes are moist. That is why dunes in Canada and Washington State are less active than dunes in Southwestern United States.

If the sand in a transverse dune becomes moist, its wavy tops break apart and the dune begins to resemble a parabolic dune. If a moist parabolic dune dries out, it turns into a barchan dune.

SAND SIZE AND WIND SPEED

If a dune's sand is fine, a gentle breeze of 8 to 12 miles (13 to 19 km) an hour can push the dune forward. About 80 percent of dune sands have medium-size grains and are moved along by winds of about 20 miles (32 km) an hour. Stronger winds—blowing at 25 to 31 miles (40 to 50 km) an hour—can lift coarse sand grains. Hurricane-force winds of 75 miles (120 km) an hour can pick up 2- to 3-inch (5- to 8-cm) rocks.

Gentle and moderate winds seldom lift blowing sand more than 24 inches (60 cm) off the ground. However, stronger winds can fling sand high and wide. The sand carried in these strong winds can cut or scar wood and metal poles.

DUNE DEVASTATION

While some dunes creep forward at a snail's pace, others are more like Olympic athletes. One Asian dune reportedly moved 60 feet (18 m) in one day. When giant dunes move quickly, they may engulf forests or bury

A snowplow? No, a "duneplow" clears the road of sand from a dune that decided to cross a road in White Sands National Monument, New Mexico. Dunes have buried houses, entire towns, and even forests.

coastal towns. For example, dunes up to 250 feet (75 m) high have buried towns along Lake Michigan.

Many years ago, the dunes of Cape Henlopen, Delaware, which travel 60 feet (18 m) a year, gobbled up a lighthouse and then consumed a nearby town. Fifty years later, some of the old buildings were exposed as the dunes continued to march forward.

Desert dunes can also destroy forests and bury villages. As dunes creep forward, deserts grow. Some desert spreading, or *desertification*, is caused by changes in Earth's climate. In many cases, however, desertification is the direct result of human activity.

The southern border of Africa's great desert, the Sahara, is a good example. In the last 20 years, it has spread 217 miles (350 km) south. Although the desertification is partially the result of drought, the damage has been worsened by people who have planted crops and grazed animals along the land bordering the desert.

Too many sheep grazing on too little land gradually destroys the pasture. As the animals uproot grass, the plants' root systems are damaged and it is harder for the soil to hold the water needed to support the plants. When the amount of grass covering an area decreases, the wind blows away more and more topsoil. Eventually all that is left are patches of sagebrush—and sand.

The Sahara, the world's largest desert, sprawls some 3,000 miles (4,828 km) from east to west. About 15 percent of the desert is covered with dunes.

Sand dunes may replace land that was once was productive. Along the southern Sahara, forests have been replaced by grasslands. As sand moved into the area, the trees died or were chopped down for firewood. Eventually the grass itself was no longer able to survive, and sand covered the entire area.

Once a large area has been overwhelmed by desert it is very difficult, if not impossible, to make it productive again. It is not uncommon for scientists digging among the Saharan dunes to uncover old irrigation ditches and other remains of ancient farming villages.

Deserts are spreading in other parts of Africa too— Botswana, Kenya, Tanzania, and Ethiopia. They are also spreading in parts of Argentina, Mexico, and the southwestern United States. As in the Sahara, desertification has been caused by unwise land use. Every year, the deserts of the world expand and take over productive land the size of the state of Maine.

For example, let's look at what happened in the huge Navajo Indian Reservation in northern Arizona and New Mexico. In the mid-1800s, travelers described it as lush meadowland. When the United States government set up the reservation for the Navajos in the late 1800s, they encouraged the Indians to become sheep farmers. The sheep and the Native Americans living on the land prospered, and sheep herds became huge.

Eventually, the herds became so large that much of the rich grasslands was overgrazed and slowly turned into desert. In the 1970s, scientists estimated that one area of the reservation could safely feed 16,000 sheep at most. But they found 11,500 Navajo people with 140,000 sheep trying to live on that land. Clearly, there is a limit to how much we can expect the land to do for us—as farmers, as sheep herders, and as cattle ranchers.

Right: Scientists have discovered thirty-one acoustic dunes in various parts of the world.

DUNES THAT GO BOOM

Jack Hereford, a prospector and mining engineer, studied sand dunes in the Mojave Desert of California for more than a dozen years. Every once in a while, he used to hike to his favorite dune, Kelso Dune. It is located at the southeastern end of a 25-mile (40-km) stretch of sand dunes called Devil's Playground.

The 2-hour climb up the long and wind-blown slope of the dune would leave anyone huffing and puffing. With each step, Hereford's legs sank shin-deep into the giant dune's dry, loose sand. Finally he reached the top—a long, sharp ridge.

Kelso Dune in the Mojave National Preserve is one of California's most famous dunes. If you know just where to stomp, you can make the dune "sing."

After catching his breath and admiring the view for a few minutes, Hereford stomped wildly and beat the ridge sand with his hands. He was trying to trigger sand slides down the slipface of the dune.

Whenever a wide section of sand slid down the slipface, Hereford said he could hear a series of loud booms that echoed across the still, silent desert. Next came loud ump-pa-pas that filled the air. According to Hereford, other sounds coming from just beneath the surface sands were like "barking seals." Meanwhile, vibrations from the sounds made the dune's peak tremble.

These strange sounds were coming from an *acoustic dune*. Scientists have discovered thirty-one acoustic dunes in various parts of the world. Legends about these unusual dunes date back more than 1,500 years. The journals of the Italian explorer Marco Polo report a booming dune. British naturalist Charles Darwin heard a dune moan during his 1835 expedition into South America's Chilean desert. No one knows exactly how these monster dunes, which rise to heights of about 700 feet (213 m), produce their sounds.

THE CASE OF SAND MOUNTAIN

Several years ago a team of three scientists set up an instrument called a *geophone* to record vibrations sent through the sand of Sand Mountain in Nevada. They also set up a microphone to record sounds sent through the air. To start moaning and squeaking sand slides on the dune's steep slope, they jumped up and down at the dune's crest and dug into the sand.

The sand boomed loudest when they furiously dug a trench with a flat-bladed shovel. They described the sound as being like "a short, low note on a cello, and remarkably pure."Although the sound lasted for less than 2 seconds, it could be heard from 100 feet (30 m) away. Digging with their hands also brought results. They described the vibrations they felt with their fingertips as like "a mild electric shock."

Next they asked themselves a question: Is there any-

Sand Mountain in Nevada is an acoustic dune that can be heard up to 100 feet (30 m) away. Scientists studied the sand of this dune to see if they could find out why the dune's sand can make the dune sound off. They couldn't.

thing about the sand of booming dunes that might be different from the sand of silent dunes? To find out, they examined both types of sand under a powerful micro-scope. They noticed that sand grains from acoustic dunes were more highly polished than grains from silent dunes. Unfortunately, this difference does not explain why some dunes go boom and others don't. Scientists are still searching for answers to this mystery.

A sand dune seems like a lifeless place. But if you observe one day and night, you will probably discover that it is the home of a number of animals and plants. These dunes are part of a group in Great Sand Dunes National Monument in Colorado.

LIFE IN SAND DUNES

5

At first glance, sand dunes may seem unable to support life. A closer look, however, will reveal a variety of plants and animals that have *adapted* to survive in this unusual habitat.

A large dune—even one that is migrating—may provide a home for thirty different *species*, of plants and animals. Poison ivy, woodbine, American holly, wild lupine, honeysuckle, and goldenrod may grow along a dune's surface, while burrowing wasps live inside. Cottontail rabbits, meadow voles, grasshoppers, and termites often live in dead trees buried underneath a dune.

ANIMAL LIFE IN A DUNE

Have you ever burned your feet on a hot, sandy beach? If you have, you may have wondered why the sand was so much hotter than the air. On a summer day, when the air temperature around a seashore dune is 85°F (30°C), the dry surface of the sandy beach may be a sizzling 120°F (48°C). The temperature difference between the air and the sand may be even greater in a desert environment.

Although some plants thrive in such heat, animals cannot—at least not for long. Most of the animals on Earth—snakes and turtles, salamanders and toads, fishes and insects—are unable to control their body temperature. The body temperatures of these animals always match their environment.

A snake's temperature is always the same as the air surrounding it. As the air around these *cold-blooded* animals heats up during the day, so does the animal. At night, the air cools—and so does the body temperature of a cold-blooded animal. Since these animals can't regulate their temperature, they must stay out of the sun during the hottest part of the day.

Birds and *mammals*, which include humans, dogs, mice, and rabbits, do not have this problem. They are *warm-blooded* animals and can maintain a constant

A desert-dwelling sidewinder rattlesnake leaves its characteristic trail of curved tracks. Among its favorite snacks is another desert animal, the kangaroo rat.

body temperature. They can shiver to warm up and sweat or pant to cool down. But, even warm blooded animals may have trouble maintaining their body temperature when it is very hot or very cold. That is why people sometimes faint on the hottest summer days, and may freeze to death when the temperature is far below freezing.

Did you ever dig your toes deep into beach sand and feel how cool the sand is only a few inches down? Animals that live in or on dunes know that the sand just beneath the

45

A kangaroo rat peeks out of its burrow. The animal is remarkably well adapted to life in the desert, especially in the way it conserves water.

surface is cooler, too. That's why they remain underground during the hottest hours of the day. These animals are active only in the early morning, in the evening, or at night.

Heat is not the only challenge dune animals face. Most of them, especially those living in desert areas, must also know how to conserve water.

The kangaroo rat, which lives in the dune country of the Sonoran, Mojave, and Colorado deserts, gets the water it needs from the seeds and vegetation that it eats. Its urine contains so little water that it turns into solid pellets when it comes into contact with the air. The kangaroo rat is a model of water conservation.

The animal uses its long powerful hind legs to bound over the fine dune sands in kangaroo hops. It can leap up to 8 feet (2. 4 m) in a single jump and can race across the sand at a speed of 20 feet (6 m) per second. Fur around the kangaroo rat's toes turn its feet into "sandshoes," which

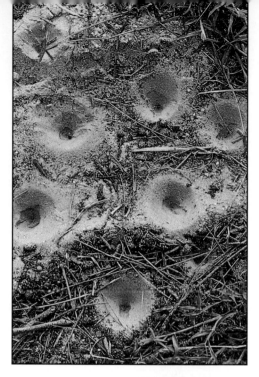

These innocent looking small pits are deadly traps made by the ant lion. Unsuspecting insects fall into the pit, slide down the loose-sand slope, and are gobbled up by the ant lion waiting below.

prevent it from sinking into the sand. Its long tail helps this animal keep its balance as it flees from enemies, such as the sidewinder rattlesnake and the kit fox.

Dunes, like other parts of the desert, often have small funnel-shaped pits—a sure sign that ant lions are around. These insects lie in wait at the bottom of their pits. When an ant or other insect tumbles down the loose sand walls, the ant lion grabs it with powerful jaws and pushes into the sand. The ant lion then paralyzes its *prey* with a poisonous fluid released from its mouth, and then eats its victim.

Desert dunes also provide a home for tiger beetles, which skip over the sand to capture and eat other insects. And there are robberflies, which suck out the body juices of their victims. Jumping spiders hunt in a catlike fashion.

Spadefoots, toads common in the southwestern deserts of the United States, are inactive for most of the year. Each year, during the brief rainy season, they emerge, mate, and then disappear underground until the next year's rain.

Most dune country of the southwestern United States has spadefoots, a type of toad. They spend 10 months of the year underground, coming to the surface only during the brief summer rains. As the water wets the desert landscape and trickles into the ground, an entire population of spadefoots suddenly appears. For a few days, they occupy every pool and puddle created by the rain. Their mating calls fill the air.

The toads mate and the females lay their eggs. Within 2 weeks, the eggs have hatched and the polliwogs have developed into adults capable of living on dry land. The young grow up just in the nick of time. Before long, the sun dries up the pools and the toads return to their underground homes in dunes or on the flat desert floor.

As you have seen, the life cycles of some dune animals depend on the coming of day and night, while others respond to seasonal change. You will soon see that the same is true for plants that live in dune habitats.

PLANT LIFE ON A DUNE

Like dune animals, dune plants use water wisely. The thin spinelike leaves of cactus plants cut down on water lost through evaporation. The fleshy stems of cactus plants store water for use in times of need.

For most of the year, the branches of the night-blooming cereus cactus are drab green-brown twigs. However, when winter rains come, small green buds appear and continue to grow through May. Then on one—and only one—night when the humidity and temperature are just right, the buds of all the cereus plants in an area burst open to reveal a beautiful, richly scented flower the size of your fist.

Then, as if by magic, sphinx moths appear, flying from one flower to another and *pollinating* the plants. This is the plants' one night of glory. Just before dawn, the

49

The beautiful flower of the cereus cactus has only one night of glory. During that night, it is pollinated by sphinx moths and makes seeds.

flowers wither, revealing a red seedpod. By sunrise, the plant once again shows only its drab green-brown color.

When greasewood plants grow on a broad dune, or surround a dune, they are often so evenly spaced that it seems as though they must have been planted. They weren't. This spacing is a result of the plant's special adaptation to a climate where water is scarce. The greasewood plant puts out shallow roots that form a 25-foot (8-m)-wide circle around the plant. This root system gives off a harmful chemical that prevents the roots of other greasewood plants from growing too close. As a result, each plant is able to grow an extensive root system and collect the water it needs.

The saguaro cactus has a deep taproot that grows straight down, as well as an extensive network of horizontal roots. The plant's horizontal roots, which may fan more than 75 feet (23 m), collect summer rainwater. The water

The fleshy stem and root system of this giant saguaro cactus is well adapted for water collection and storage.

collected by the horizontal roots is stored in the taproot and used during times of water shortage. The taproot also anchors the plant.

Some dune plants, such as the smoke bush, have tough seeds that need exactly the right amount of moisture to sprout. In some cases, the seeds lie on the ground for years. Eventually, during a fierce storm, the rushing water of flash floods picks up the seeds and dashes them against the sand and rocks. Some become trapped in crannies in the streambed, and water soaks into the seeds through cracks created during their violent journey. Only then does the seed germinate and a new plant begin to grow.

As you learned in Chapter 2, dune vegetation helps the dune to grow even larger. The plant roots hold the sand in place. In addition, the plant cover increases the dune's ability to slow the wind and alter its direction. As a result, the wind drops its cargo of flying sand on top of the dune, further enlarging it.

DUNE ECOSYSTEMS

Together, dune plants and animals form dune communities, or *ecosystems*. Thecreatures living in any ecosystem depend on each other. Plants use energy from the sun to build new branches and leaves. When an animal such as the kangaroo rat eats the seeds or fruit of these plants, it is able to grow, too.

Plants, in turn, depend on animals. The seeds of some dune plants cannot sprout until they are collected by a sand rat. The rats carry the seeds into their dune burrows, where they eat some and store the rest. Some of these stored seeds sprout, push up through the sand, and grow along the surface of the dune.

In many cases, the location of a dune—desert, lake, or seacoast—determines the kinds of creatures that live

This small pond amid the dunes of Michigan's Warren Dunes State Park affects the kinds of dune animals and plants that can live there. As a source of moisture, the pond also contributes to the moisture content of the sand, which in turn affects how a dune behaves.

there. The landscape often dictates how the organisms interact.

During periods of strong winds, insects living in and around the Indiana dunes along Lake Michigan are blown into the lake and drown. Their bodies are soon returned to the beach by the tide. Shorebirds feed on the dead insects, and so does an insect called the fiery searcher beetle. In a desert area, insects overpowered by winds would never be returned to the community to become a source of food for other animals.

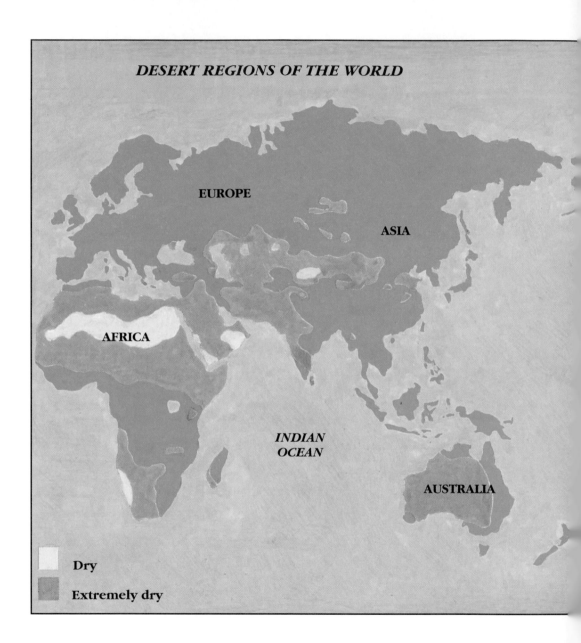

DESERT REGIONS OF THE WORLD

6

NORTH
AMERICA

PACIFIC
OCEAN

SOUTH
AMERICA

Desert covers much of the Middle East, affecting such countries as Iraq, Iran, Saudi Arabia, and Israel. Some of the world's highest sand dunes are in Iraq and Iran. Deserts also cover parts of India and China as well as most of northern Africa and Australia.

There are also many dune areas in North and South America. Many South American deserts lie along the Pacific Coast where the mighty Andes mountain chain drains the moist winds blowing off the ocean. More than half of South America's west coast is extremely arid.

SAND DUNES OF NORTH AMERICA

Name	Location	Characteristics
DEVIL'S PLAYGROUND MOJAVE DESERT	Southeast of Baker, California	Some of the highest dunes in the United States
GEORGIAN DUNES	Along the eastern shore of the Little Ohoopee, Canoochee, Altamaha, and Savannah rivers in Georgia	Largest individual dunes are nearly 5 miles (8 km) long, 2 miles (3 km) wide, and 100 feet (30 m) high; one-of-a kind desert-type dunes in found high above the flood-plains of inland streams
INDIANA DUNES STATE PARK	East of Chicago between Gary and Michigan City	A 4-mile (6-km) stretch of dunes backed by forests and bogs; play area that offers many lessons in the ecology of sand dunes
LANPHERE-CHRISTENSEN DUNES	Near Eureka, California	233 acres (94 ha) of coastal dunes up to 50 feet (15 m) high; among the best examples of sand dune evolution on the west coast of the United States; a colorful blanket of wild flowers makes the dunes espesially attractive in spring
OREGON DUNES NATIONAL RECREATION AREA	From the Siuslaw River to Coos Bay in Oregon	Includes some 18,000 aces (7,285 ha) of coastal dunes; European beach grass has allowed a long barrier dune to form; older sprawling dunes up to 2 miles (3 km) inland receive no new sand

SAND DUNES OF NORTH AMERICA (continued)

Name	Location	Characteristics
RICHARDSON RIVER SAND HILLS	Lake Athabasca area of Alberta, Canada	Some of the most spectacular dunes in Canada
ST. ANTHONY SAND DUNES	West of St. Anthony, Idaho	Area seems like a miniature version of the Sahara; dunes are 200 to 300 feet (60 to 90 m) high and 1 to 5 miles (1.6 to 8 km) wide; very fine sand that packs well when wet, so that vehicles can be used to explore the dunes
WARREN DUNES PARK	Near Bridgman, Michigan	Among the world's largest lakeshore dunes; includes huge parabolic dunes and barrier dunes with steep windward slopes caused by storm waves; site of a large *blowout*
WHITE SANDS NATIONAL MONUMENT	Southwest of Alamogordo, New Mexico	World's largest gypsum desert; mile after mile of high shifting dunes with gleaming white sands
WYOMING DUNES	South of Eden, Wyoming	Largest dune area in the United States; not well known because it is hard to reach

Perhaps the largest dune area in the United States lies south of Eden, Wyoming. These dunes stretch for more than 100 miles (160 km). Indiana, Nebraska, New Mexico, Michigan, Colorado, and California also have spectacular dune country. Michigan's Sleeping Bear Dune rises 450 feet (137 m); southern Colorado dunes top 600 feet (183 m); and some California dunes are even higher.

Dunes can also be found in southern Alaska, Delaware, Massachusetts, New Jersey, North Carolina, Oregon, Texas, and Long Island, New York. If you would like to learn more about dunes in your area, you can write to a local Geological Survey. The agency is there to serve you and will be happy to send you all sorts of information.

GLOSSARY

acoustic dune—a large sand dune that moans, booms, or makes other sounds when energetic sandslides occur on the slip-face. Some thirty-one acoustic dunes have been identified.

adapt—to change and, as a result, better meet the demands of the environment. A plant or animal population's adaptations help it deal with problems, including scarcity of food and change in climate.

barchan dune—a crescent-shaped dune with "horns" that face away from the predominant wind. Barchan dunes are usually 30 to 100 feet (9 to 30 m) high.

barrier dune—a dune that forms when wind-blown sand piles up along a beach front. The dune acts like a seawall that pro tects houses and trees along the shore against storm waves and flood tides. (Also called foredunes.)

basalt—hardened lava. Basalt sands cover some of the world's beaches.

blowout—an opening in a barrier dune that allows sand to be blown into dunes far inland.

calcite—a common mineral compound made of calcium carbon- ate. Limestone, marble, chalk, and seashells consist largely of calcite. Broken calcite shells form some of the world's beaches.

cold-blooded—having a body temperature that changes with the temperature of the environment.

desertification—the gradual covering over of an area by sand, sometimes brought on by mismanagement of the land.

face—one side or slope of a dune.

fulgurite—a slender, usually tubelike body of glassy rock. It forms when lightning strikes and melts dry sand. When the sand solidifies, individual grains fuse together.

ecosystem—a group of organisms living in an envi-ronment with specific physical conditions.

geophone—an electronic receiver used to detect earthquake waves.

gypsum—a white or yellowish mineral. Gypsum sand covers some of the world's beaches.

lime tube—a calcite coating that may form around the stem of a dune plant.

longitudinal dune—dunes that form long ridges in the direc-tion the wind is blowing. These dunes are often quite long.

mammals—warm-blooded higher vertebrates that nourish their young with milk.

organism—any living thing.

parabolic dune—a long dune with a U-shaped crest. The long "arms" of these dunes may be anchored by vegetation or mois-ture while their curved end is blown longer.

phytogenic dune—dunes with grasses and other plants.

pollinate—to transfer pollen from the anther (male part of the flower) to the stigma (female part of the flower).

prey—an animal that is hunted for food.

quartz—a very hard mineral made of silica and found in sev-eral rock types, including sandstone and granite. The sand in most of the world's dunes is made primarily of quartz sand.

sand dune—a mound of sand that is created and shaped by the wind.

silicon dioxide—the chemical compound known as silica, or sand.

slipface—the steep face of a dune that forms on the lee, or down-wind, side of the dune.

slope—one side or face of a dune.

species—a group of organisms that produce viable offspring when they mate.

s-shaped dune—a dune shaped like the letter "S." It forms when winds of equal intensity blow from opposite directions.

star-shaped dune—a dune that is shaped by winds from several different directions. The bases of these dunes resemble a many-pointed star.

transverse dune—sand dunes formed by fine sand blown by winds from a single direction. Transverse dunes are more common inland from beaches than in deserts.

warm blooded—animals, including mammals and birds, that can maintain a constant body temperature, regardless of the temperature of their surroundings. Such animals have a survival advantage over cold-blooded animals.

INDEX

FOR FURTHER READING

Hamilton, William J., III. "The Living Sands of the Nambi." *National Geographic.* September 1983, 364–377.

Lancaster, Nicholas. "Development of Kelso Dunes." *National Geographic Research & Exploration.* Autumn 1993, 444–459.

Vesilind, Priit J. "The Sonoran Desert." *National Geographic.* September 1994, 36–63.

ABOUT THE AUTHOR

Roy A. Gallant has been called "one of the deans of American science writers for children" by *School Library Journal.* He has written more than eighty books for children on topics including astronomy, earth science, and evolution.

Gallant has worked at the American Museum of Natural History and been a member of the faculty of New York City's Hayden Planetarium. He is currently the director of the Southworth Planetarium at the University of Southern Maine, where he also holds an adjunct full professorship.